WORLD'S FAVORITE CLASSIC TO CONTEMPORARY PIANO MUSIC

EARLY GRADE
PIANO MUSIC
IN ITS
ORIGINAL FORM

SELECTED
AND
COMPILED BY

MARIE HILL

FOREWORD

This book answers the demand, so often expressed in teaching circles, for relatively simple music which gives the form and style of the masters, without distortion or alteration of any kind.

The content of this volume was carefully chosen, particularly to show the style of each composer and to give a chronological picture of the early classics, the Baroque period, the romantic school, leading up to the modern school.

The music provides, for each composer represented, a spread of difficulty and a diversity of style, which permits the teacher to choose material suited to students in various stages of progress. In a few instances, only one composition of the composer is chosen, as being representative of his style.

MARIE HILL has studied with Tobias Matthay, in England, and with Josef and Rosina Lhevinne at the Juilliard Graduate School, has devoted many years to the field of piano instruction, and has written numerous text books used by music schools throughout the nation.

We are indeed proud to present this unusual musical collection, and we feel it will make a substantial contribution to the field of music teaching and music appreciation.

The Publisher

© Copyright 1961 by
ASHLEY PUBLICATIONS, INC,
263 Veterans Blvd., Carlstadt, N.J. 07072
International Copyright Secured   Made in U.S.A.

CONTENTS

(In Chronological Sequence by Composers' Dates of Birth)

©Copyright 1961 by **ASHLEY PUBLICATIONS, INC.** • 263 Veterans Blvd., Carlstadt, N.J. 07072

International Copyright Secured   *Made in U.S.A.*   *All Rights Reserved, Including Public Performance for Profit*

CONTENTS

ALPHABETIC INDEX TO COMPOSERS

For Convenient Alphabetic Title Index See Page 160

Air

HENRY PURCELL (1658-1695)

Allegretto grazioso

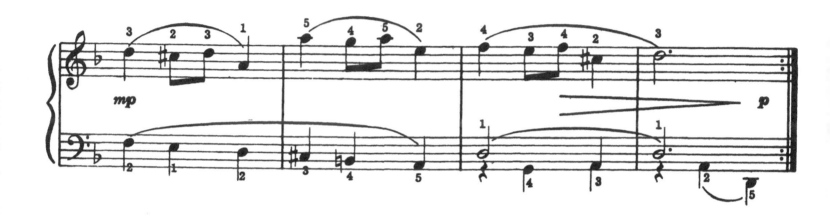

©Copyright 1961 by **ASHLEY PUBLICATIONS, INC.** • 263 Veterans Blvd., Carlstadt, N.J. 07072

International Copyright Secured   *Made in U.S.A.*   *All Rights Reserved, Including Public Performance for Profit*

Rigadoon

HENRY PURCELL

Animato

Hornpipe in E Minor

Allegro

HENRY PURCELL

Trumpet Call
(Intrada)

Allegro

HENRY PURCELL

Aria

FRANÇOIS COUPERIN (1668 - 1733)

8

Gavotte

Allegro

FRANCOIS COUPERIN

Miniature

FRANCOIS COUPERIN

Tempo di Minuetto

The Cuckoos

FRANCOIS COUPERIN

Allegretto

Minuet

JEAN PHILIPPE RAMEAU (1683 - 1764)

Minuet in G Minor

Allegro moderato

JEAN PHILIPPE RAMEAU

Tender Complaints

Rondo

JEAN PHILIPPE RAMEAU

Andantino

1st Couplet

Refrain

Tambourin

JEAN PHILIPPE RAMEAU

Minuetto in Bb Major

DOMENICO SCARLATTI (1683 - 1757)

Moderato

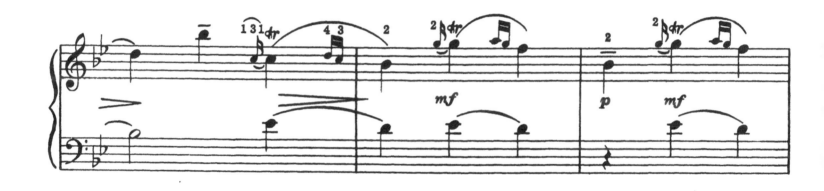

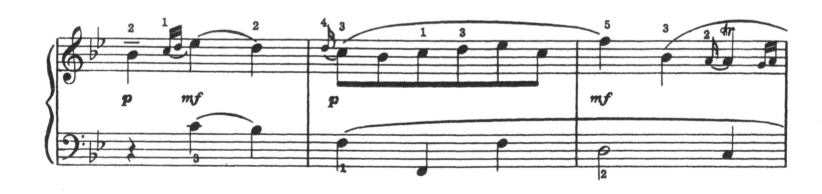

Larghetto in D Minor

DOMENICO SCARLATTI

Allegro in D Major

DOMENICO SCARLATTI

Allegro

Chorale
(Do as Thou will'st me, O Lord!)

JOHANN SEBASTIAN BACH (1685 - 1750)

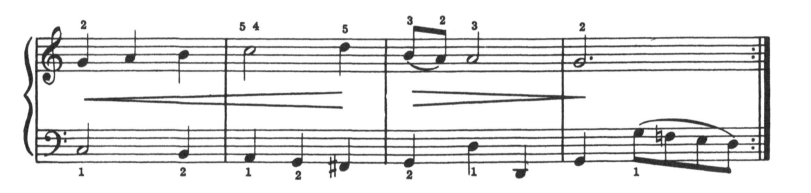

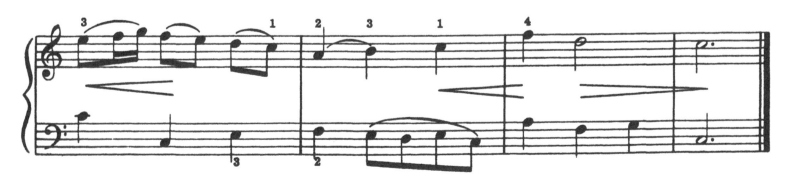

Chorale
(What joy is mine, O Friend of mortals)

JOHANN SEBASTIAN BACH

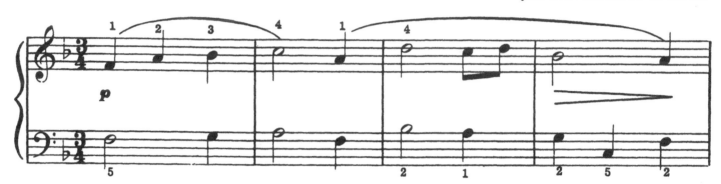

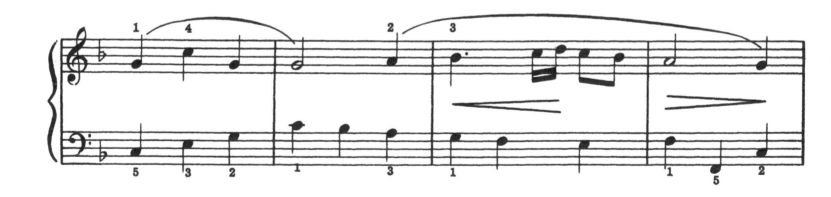

Minuet in G Major

Allegretto

JOHANN SEBASTIAN BACH

Minuet in G Minor

Allegretto

JOHANN SEBASTIAN BACH

March in D Major

JOHANN SEBASTIAN BACH

Allegro maestoso

Musette in D Major

Allegro con brio

JOHANN SEBASTIAN BACH

Minuet in D Minor

Andante

JOHANN SEBASTIAN BACH

Little Prelude in C

Allegro non troppo

JOHANN SEBASTIAN BACH

Polonaise in G Minor

JOHANN SEBASTIAN BACH

Minuet in F No. 1

GEORGE FREDERIC HANDEL (1685 - 1759)

Minuet in F No. 2

GEORGE FREDERIC HANDEL

Andantino

Courante

GEORGE FREDERIC HANDEL

Impertinence

GEORGE FREDERIC HANDEL

Allegro

Little Dance

FRANZ JOSEPH HAYDN (1732 - 1809)

Allegro in F Major

FRANZ JOSEPH HAYDN

Allegro

Dance in G Major

FRANZ JOSEPH HAYDN

Allegretto

Minuetto Giocoso

FRANZ JOSEPH HAYDN

The Miller

GIOVANNI PAISIELLO (1740 - 1816)

Minuet in F

WOLFGANG AMADEUS MOZART (1756 - 1791)

Minuet in C

WOLFGANG AMADEUS MOZART

Moderato

Arietta

WOLFGANG AMADEUS MOZART

Andante

Allegro in Bb

WOLFGANG AMADEUS MOZART

Andantino

Andantino

WOLFGANG AMADEUS MOZART

Polonaise

WOLFGANG AMADEUS MOZART

Ecossaise in G

LUDWIG VAN BEETHOVEN (1770 - 1827)

German Dance

LUDWIG VAN BEETHOVEN

Ecossaise in Eb

LUDWIG VAN BEETHOVEN

Allegro con brio

Country Dance

Allegretto

LUDWIG VAN BEETHOVEN

Sonatina in G

LUDWIG VAN BEETHOVEN

Moderato

ROMANZE

Valse Sentimentale

FRANZ SCHUBERT (1797 - 1828)

Waltz in G

FRANZ SCHUBERT

Waltz in F

FRANZ SCHUBERT

Moderato

Waltz in D

Allegretto non troppo

FRANZ SCHUBERT

Venetian Boat Song No. 2

Allegretto tranquillo

FELIX MENDELSSOHN (1809 - 1847)

Soldier's March

Allegro deciso

ROBERT SCHUMANN (1810 - 1856)

The Wild Horseman

ROBERT SCHUMANN

Allegro con brio

The Happy Farmer

ROBERT SCHUMANN

Allegretto

Waltz

Animato

ROBERT SCHUMANN

Berceuse

STEPHEN HELLER (1815 - 1888)

Avalanche

Allegro vivace

STEPHEN HELLER

The Doll's Lament

Andantino

CESAR FRANCK (1822 - 1890)

German Song

Tranquillo

PETER ILICH TSCHAIKOWSKY (1840 - 1893)

Italian Song

PETER ILICH TSCHAIKOWSKY

Moderato

Waltz in E Flat

P. I. TSCHAIKOWSKY

Allegro moderato

Cowherd's Song

EDVARD GRIEG (1843 - 1907)

Album Leaf

Allegretto

EDVARD GRIEG

To a Wild Rose

EDWARD Mac DOWELL (1861 - 1908)

With simple tenderness

Valsette

JAN SIBELIUS
1865 - 1957

A Little Waltz

RHENE-BATON
1879 - 1940

Two Folk Songs

Simply

BELA BARTOK (1881 - 1945)

BELA BARTOK

Fast and bright

Children at Play

Simply

BELA BARTOK

Folk Dance

BELA BARTOK

Folk Dance

BELA BARTOK

Allegretto scherzando

Sad Song

BELA BARTOK

Step Lively

BELA BARTOK

Two Folk Tunes

BELA BARTOK

Allegro

II.

March

SERGE PROKOFIEFF (1891-1953)

Tempo di Marcia

A Happy Fairy Tale

SERGE PROKOFIEFF

Morning

Andante tranquillo

SERGE PROKOFIEFF

Regrets

SERGE PROKOFIEFF

Ivan Sings

ARAM KHACHATURIAN (1903-)

Running Along

A Little Scherzo

DMITRI KABALEVSKY (1904 -)

Galloping

DMITRI KABALEVSKY

A Gay Little Story

DMITRI KABALEVSKY

Briskly

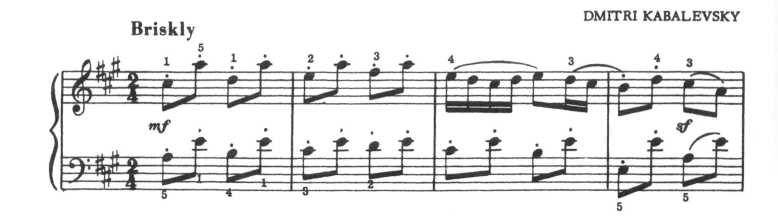

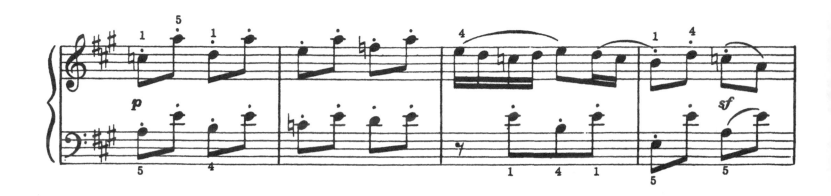

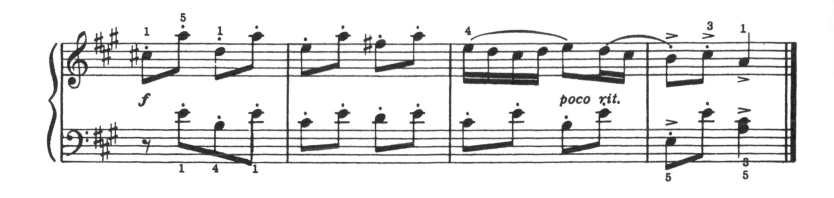

Hopping

DMITRI KABALEVSKY

Fast, with great energy

Waltz

Slowly and quietly

DMITRI KABALEVSKY

Tempo I

Having Fun

DMITRI KABALEVSKY

Waltz

DMITRI SHOSTAKOVICH (1906-)

March

DMITRI SHOSTAKOVICH

Tempo di Marcia

A Happy Fairy Tale

DMITRI SHOSTAKOVICH

The Mechanical Doll

DMITRI SHOSTAKOVICH

Allegretto

ALPHABETICAL TITLE INDEX

ALPHABETICAL TITLE INDEX